License to Life: 21 Lessons I Learned Growing Up — and How They Guide My Life

ISBN (Paperback): 979-8-9941236-0-7
ISBN (Hardcover): 979-8-9941236-1-4

This book is a work of nonfiction. Names, places, and events are described as accurately as possible. Some details may have been changed to protect privacy. Any resemblance to actual persons, living or deceased, or actual events is coincidental.

The views and opinions expressed in this book are those of the author and do not necessarily reflect the views of any organization or employer.

This book is not intended as legal, medical, or professional advice. Readers are encouraged to seek appropriate professional guidance when needed.

Printed in the United States of America

LICENSE TO LIFE

**21 Lessons I Learned Growing Up
– and How They Guide My Life**

by Tacuma Stanfield

DEDICATION

This book is dedicated to the people who shaped me,
strengthened me, and guided me.
To my wife — thank you for your love and partnership.
To my children — you are my purpose and my joy.
To my parents — your wisdom carried me farther than you know.
To my brothers and my entire Stanfield and Johnson family —
thank you for the foundation you gave me.

And to my cousin, **Quintin Levingston**
— gone too soon in 2025.
Your life, your spirit, and your legacy inspired
me to finish this book.
This is for us.

ABOUT THE AUTHOR

Tacuma Stanfield was born in Riverside, California and now resides in Atlanta, Georgia. A proud graduate of Clark Atlanta University, Tacuma is a husband, father, leader, and mentor who believes in the power of growth through experience. His passion is pouring wisdom into others — from young adults to established leaders — and helping people discover the best version of themselves. He enjoys sports, travel, and creating impact in every community he touches.

CONTENTS

CHAPTER 1 — Protect Your Brothers at All Costs　　13

CHAPTER 2 — Never Say You Can't　　21

CHAPTER 3 — You Have Two Ears: Listen Before You Speak　　27

CHAPTER 4 — Work Hard, Play Hard　　33

CHAPTER 5 — Always Be On Time　　39

CHAPTER 6 — Never Quit　　45

CHAPTER 7 — Always Be There for Your Kids　　53

CHAPTER 8 — Do What You Say You're Going to Do　　59

CHAPTER 9 — Your Image Matters　　65

CHAPTER 10 — Treat Others How You Want to Be Treated　　73

CHAPTER 11 — Never Follow the Joneses　　81

CHAPTER 12 — Nothing in Life Is Free　　87

CHAPTER 13 — Return What You Borrow in Better Condition　　93

CHAPTER 14 — Clean Up After Yourself　　101

CHAPTER 15 — When Ironing a Dress Shirt,
　　　　　　　Start Behind the Collar　　107

CHAPTER 16 — You Can Do It (Don't Project Onto Others)　　115

CHAPTER 17 — We All Bleed Red　　123

CHAPTER 18 — Open the Door for Your Spouse　　131

CHAPTER 19 — Meet People Where They Are　　139

CHAPTER 20 — Inspect What You Expect　　147

CHAPTER 21 — Finish Strong　　155

INTRODUCTION —
21 Lessons I Learned Growing Up

There are moments in life when you look back and realize every lesson, every scar, every mistake, every blessing, and every conversation shaped the person you became. For me, those lessons started early — in a home filled with brothers, discipline, laughter, competition, and love. Some lessons were loud and direct. Others were quiet, tucked inside small moments, fully understood only years later. But all of them mattered.

I didn't grow up with everything, but I grew up with enough — enough structure, enough wisdom, enough love, and enough real-life experiences to understand the world differently. My parents, poured into me the best way they knew how. My brothers tough-ened me up, challenged me, protected me, and forced me to grow. My community, from Riverside to Compton to Atlanta, shaped my iden-tity and humbled me. And as a man, a husband, a father, a leader, and a believer in people, I've learned that the most powerful lessons are often the simplest ones.

This book is not written from the mountaintop — it's written from the climb. I don't have all the answers. I've made mistakes, taken losses, quit things I should have finished, finished things I should have quit, and learned from all of it. I've seen hard moments break people, and I've seen other people take the same pain and turn it into something beautiful. What I do know is this: lessons don't expire. They show up differently at every stage of your life, but the truth remains the same.

The 21 lessons in this book come from real stories — my childhood, my parents, my brothers, my career, my relationships, my failures, my wins, my fears, and my growth. These are lessons that guided me and lessons I hope will guide someone else, whether you're a parent, a young man trying to figure it out, a leader searching for purpose, or someone standing at a crossroads wondering what comes next.

I wrote this book for the people who weren't handed everything.
For the people navigating life with memory, instinct, and faith.
For the people who understand that growth is a process.
For the people who need a push, a reminder, or a little bit of guidance.
For the people who never heard enough "you can do it."

And I wrote it for my daughters — because I want them to know the lessons that raised me, and the lessons I hope will strengthen them.

Each chapter is short, honest, and straight to the point.
Some will challenge you.
Some will feel familiar.
Some might sting a little.
All of them are real.

This is my story, but it's also yours — because somewhere in these pages, you'll find yourself.

Let's begin.

CHAPTER 1

PROTECT YOUR BROTHERS AT ALL COSTS

Core Lesson: Loyalty is non-negotiable

Loyalty was the very first lesson I ever learned. Not because someone sat me down and explained it, but because life itself demanded it. Growing up with three brothers meant one thing: *we were responsible for each other.* If one fought, we all fought. If one was disrespected, we all felt it. And if I ever found out a brother didn't stand up for another — well, that was going to be a whole different problem.

But protecting your brothers wasn't just about throwing hands. It was about valuing the people who value you. It was about showing up. It was about loyalty in its purest form — the type that doesn't need to be announced or explained. The type that's lived.

THE TIRE INCIDENT

I remember being about eight years old, playing with the neighborhood kids while my dad washed his car. And let me tell you — my pops' cars were always immaculate. The shine on his tires looked like glass. That man treated those cars like they were royalty.

We came back to the house after playing, and while everyone was drinking from the water hose like kids did back then, my friend decided — for whatever reason — to haul off and kick my dad's tire. A clean, shiny, freshly dressed tire.

That was it.

In that moment, it wasn't about the tire. It wasn't even about the car. It was about respect. And if you disrespected something my father cared about, you were disrespecting my father — which meant you were disrespecting my family. I had to defend that. I fought my friend not out of anger, but out of loyalty. Out of protection. Out of something deeper that was already being built in me at a young age.

BROTHERHOOD GOES BEYOND FIGHTING

As I got older, I realized protection wasn't always physical. Sometimes protecting someone meant stopping a fight, not starting one.

I remember being in middle school, and word got around that someone wanted to fight me during lunch. My brother — only eleven months older — heard what was going on from across the field. He didn't ask questions. He didn't hesitate. He ran over, stepped in, and shut everything down before it escalated.

That moment taught me something important:
Loyalty is not always about throwing punches.
Sometimes it's about preventing them.

Sometimes protecting your brother means putting him in a position where he doesn't have to fight at all.

That's a lesson I carry today — in life, in friendships, and especially in leadership.

LEAVING TOGETHER MEANS RETURNING TOGETHER

Protecting your brothers at all costs also meant staying together.
If we left the house together, we returned to the house together. No exceptions.

That rule played out countless times growing up. Back then, it was simple. We needed each other for protection, security, and guidance, so sticking together wasn't questioned—it was standard. But as we got older and began forming our own friendships and social circles, that rule became harder to live by.

During my high school years, I relocated to Georgia to live with my father, while one of my brothers remained in California with my mother. He was slightly older than me, so he finished high school first and eventually moved to Georgia to live with us as well. Once I settled in, I made new friends and naturally began introducing my brother to many of them.

My brother drove a 1969 Volkswagen Beetle—purchased for one dollar from our much older stepbrother. It wasn't flashy or reliable, but it was his. He used it primarily to get back and forth from college and work.

One night, some friends from my high school—who happened to be the same age as my brother—threw a party at an old skating rink near where I went to school. My brother was off work that day, so I asked if he wanted to go. Him coming along also meant I could stay out later, because my brother's curfew automatically became my curfew.

After the party, a few of my friends had what we thought was a great idea at the time—getting a hotel room in Clayton County with some of our girlfriends. My brother's Volkswagen didn't have much room, and certainly not enough space for all of us, so I decided to ride with a friend who had a newer, more reliable car.

As we drove toward the hotel, I wasn't paying much attention. At some point, my brother's car couldn't keep up with the pace we were going. I didn't realize it at the time—I only noticed once we arrived.

That's when it hit me.

We weren't old enough to be at a hotel to begin with, but that wasn't my biggest concern. I had no idea where my brother was. I didn't know if his car broke down, if he missed the exit, or if he even knew how to get there. This was a time when cell phones were a luxury—none of my friends had one. GPS didn't exist. Once you lost someone, they were simply gone.

I couldn't enjoy anything after that.

Worried and anxious, I told—more accurately, demanded—that a friend take me home. I knew the rule. When you leave together, you return together. And I knew I had broken it.

When I got home, my brother wasn't there. I thought he'd be waiting for me. That made the pit in my stomach even worse.

I walked inside, and my dad asked a simple question:
"Where's your brother?"

I didn't lie.

I told him everything—the party, the hotel idea, leaving my brother behind. I owned it. I was scared, disappointed in myself, and fully expecting the consequences. That night reinforced a lesson I already knew but clearly needed reminded of: at all costs, you stick together.

What I didn't know at the time was that my brother had safely made it to our other brother's house. My dad already knew. He wasn't testing my whereabouts—he was testing my integrity.

Would I tell the truth, or would I lie?

I told the truth.

That moment stayed with me. Loyalty isn't just about protection in the moment—it's about responsibility, accountability, and honesty when you fall short. That night reminded me that brotherhood isn't optional, and integrity is proven when it's uncomfortable.

And it was a lesson I never forgot.

LOYALTY IN LEADERSHIP

In my career, I've managed teams, built strategy, and carried the weight of decisions that impact other people's livelihoods. And what I've learned is this:

A real leader protects their team.

Sometimes upper leadership sets a strategy that you know could be improved. But as a leader, you roll it out anyway — because alignment matters. Then you tell your team:

"If this doesn't work, I'll take the blame.
If it succeeds, the credit goes to you."

That's loyalty.
That's brotherhood.
That's protecting your people in a different arena.

It's the same lesson from childhood, just applied in boardrooms instead of backyards.

LOYALTY IS BIGGER THAN THE MOMENT

Loyalty is trust.
Loyalty is respect.
Loyalty is honor.

Loyalty is standing up for people even when they don't know you're standing up for them.

In the neighborhood, loyalty meant you never snitched, you never folded, and you always respected the crew. But as an adult, loyalty grows. It becomes more mature, more strategic, more purpose-driven.

Today, loyalty shows up in how you love your family, how you show up for friends, how you lead a team, and how you establish your character in every environment you touch.

Protecting your brothers at all costs isn't about fighting.
It's about valuing the people who value you.
It's about standing firm even when no one's watching.
It's about choosing integrity over convenience.

Because loyalty — real loyalty — never goes out of style.

CHAPTER 2

NEVER SAY YOU CAN'T

Core Lesson: The words you speak shape the limits you believe.

Some lessons in life are spoken. Others are enforced.
"Never say you can't" was both in our household.

Growing up, both of my parents made one rule very clear: we were never allowed to say *"I can't."*

That phrase didn't live in our house. It didn't matter if it was schoolwork, chores, sports, or something new we were trying—the moment you said "I can't," you got corrected instantly.

As kids, of course we all had moments where we *felt* like we couldn't do something. But feeling something and it being true are two very different things. My parents always reminded us:

"I can't becomes real only when you make it real."

They understood something most people don't learn until much later in life: once you let a limitation come out of your mouth, it settles in your mind. And once it settles in your mind, it becomes your truth—even when it's not.

This lesson started small, but it grew with me. It continues to grow even today. That's why the words you speak matter. You can talk yourself out of your own potential faster than the world ever could.

THE CORNBREAD & MILK MOMENT

Every kid has a favorite snack. Mine?

Cornbread and milk — warm cornbread broken up in a bowl with just the right amount of milk poured over it. Heaven.

One day when I was about six, I wanted some, so I went looking for help. My brothers wouldn't make it for me, so I went to my mom. She looked at me and said:

"*You do it.*"

I told her, "*I can't.*"

She turned to me with that look only a mother can give — part love, part correction.

"You can. And I'll show you how, so next time you can do it on your own."

She took me into the kitchen. Had me climb on the counter to get a bowl. Showed me how to warm the cornbread for 30 seconds.Showed me how much milk to pour.

And just like that, I learned I could do something I had convinced myself I couldn't. That small moment planted the seed of independence, confidence, and self-belief.

Never say you can't — because sometimes all you need is an example.

LOSING MY VISION — AND LOSING MY CONFIDENCE

Years later, life tested this lesson in a much deeper way.

In my early 20s — right at the end of my first semester of college — I woke up one morning feeling like I had an eyelash stuck in my eye. Annoying, but manageable. But over the next few days, the irritation turned into pain, and the pain turned into darkness.

Within weeks, I could barely see.

An optometrist sent me to a specialist, and after running tests, the doctor told me I was experiencing **vitreous hemorrhaging**. They used lasers to stop the bleeding, but the damage had already been done. My retina tore. I lost sight in my left eye.

That moment broke my confidence.
I didn't feel like myself.
I questioned everything.

I told myself I couldn't approach a woman.
I couldn't play basketball.
I couldn't get certain jobs.
I couldn't be who I was before.

"I can't" started creeping back into my life — silently, slowly, and consistently.

But here's the thing about being surrounded by the right people:
They don't let you quit on yourself.
They remind you who you are.
They pull you back into the light when you can't see it.

Piece by piece, I learned to trust myself again. And eventually, I learned something important:

Confidence can be rebuilt.
Sight may not return — but identity can.

THE WIRELESS JOB THAT CHANGED EVERYTHING

Not long after recovering, I applied for a retail sales consultant job at a major wireless carrier. I was nervous. Really nervous.

I was the new guy.
Never sold anything before.
Didn't know how to take the back off a Nokia 3390 to save my life.

My first customer needed help, and even though I made the sale, it wasn't because of my skill — it was because they needed the phone more than I knew what I was doing.

I was sweating, fumbling, struggling... and my manager watched the whole thing.

After the transaction, he pulled me aside. And instead of criticizing me, he coached me:

- How to stand tall
- How to greet a customer with confidence
- How to ask open-ended and closed-ended questions
- How to lead the conversation
- How to take control of the moment instead of shrinking in it

He role-played with me.
Poured into me.
Believed in me.

My second customer walked in later that day.
I used everything he taught me.

That customer came in for two phones — they left with five.

That moment changed my career.
It taught me how to sell, how to lead, and how to carry myself in any room.

But it also taught me this:
Sometimes "I can't" isn't spoken.
Sometimes it shows up in your posture, your voice, your hesitation.
Confidence isn't just a mindset — it's a behavior.

YOU CAN DO MORE THAN YOU THINK

This chapter is not about pretending life is easy.
It's about understanding that challenges don't disqualify you — they shape you.

You may lose something along the way.
You may struggle.
You may doubt.

But as long as you stay teachable, stay open, and stay in motion, you can rebuild anything you lose — confidence, momentum, habits, direction.

The truth is simple:
You can do it.
Even when you don't believe it yet.
Especially then.**

TAKEAWAY

Never say you can't — because you might be standing one lesson, one person, one moment away from realizing that you always could.

CHAPTER 3

LISTEN BEFORE YOU SPEAK

Core Lesson: You learn more for listening than you ever will from talking.

Growing up, listening wasn't just a suggestion — it was a survival skill. Anytime I tried to talk myself out of a whoopin, my father would give me that look: *"If you would've listened, we wouldn't be here right now."*

He wasn't wrong.

After the punishment — once the tears dried and the room calmed — my father always explained *why* we got disciplined. He didn't believe in letting a lesson go unnamed. He wanted us to understand what we did wrong so we wouldn't repeat it.

Looking back, that was the earliest version of this lesson: **If you don't listen, you can't grow. If you don't know where you stand, you can't make corrections.**

Listening is corrective.
Listening is protective.
Listening is maturity.

It's a skill that will save you more pain than discipline ever could.

LISTENING IS LIKE MUSIC TO YOUR SOUL

You learn more from listening than you ever will from talking. People reveal their wisdom, their experiences, their intentions, and their hearts when you choose to be quiet long enough to hear them.

Listening has shaped my entire life.

It has grounded my relationships, guided my career, and built my character.

And in a world where everyone is talking, posting, venting, and arguing — listening is becoming a lost art. But it's also one of the greatest advantages you can have.

WHEN YOU DON'T LISTEN, YOU MISS WHAT MATTERS

In relationships, listening is everything.

I've seen it in my own marriage.

There are moments when my wife comes to me with thoughts, concerns, or emotions she wants to express. And sometimes, if I react too quickly, I miss the meaning behind her words. When you interrupt, you don't just cut off the sentence — you cut off the connection.

Most relationships fail not because people stop loving each other, but because they stop *listening* to each other.

Listening creates safety.

Safety creates trust.
Trust creates longevity.

It's the same with friendships, your children, and even people you've dated in the past. If you care about someone, you listen to them.

LISTENING AT WORK IS A SUPERPOWER

In the workplace, people told me during annual reviews that I should "speak up more." But I've always believed the opposite:

Listening is actually being the most outspoken in the room.

When you listen:

- You catch details other people miss
- You understand the real problem behind the problem
- You speak with clarity because you waited to gather information
- Your voice carries more weight when you finally choose to speak

Some people talk just to be heard.
Others speak with purpose because they listened first.

Those are the people who move organizations.
Those are the people others follow.

Listening is strategy.

MY NAME MEANS 'ALERT' —
AND LISTENING IS PART OF THAT

My name, **Tacuma**, means *alert*.

Growing up, I always paid attention — to the room, to the energy, to people's behavior. My friends still tell me they feel safe around me because I'm always aware, always observing, always listening.

Listening isn't just something I do — it's who I am.
It's part of my identity.
It's the reason I navigate life the way I do.

LISTENING KEEPS YOU OUT OF TROUBLE — AND PUTS YOU IN POSITION

Life has shown me two kinds of people:
1. Those who listen and move wisely
2. Those who talk themselves into avoidable mistakes

Silence is underrated.
Observing the room is underrated.
Understanding before responding is underrated.

Listening gives you access to opportunities, relationships, and respect that talking could never earn.

TAKEAWAY

Listening isn't passive — it's power.
When you listen, you learn.
When you listen, you connect.
When you listen, you protect your peace and elevate your path.

Because the truth is simple:

God gave you two ears and one mouth for a reason.
Use them in that order.

CHAPTER 4

WORK HARD, PLAY HARD

Core Lesson: You earn your joy by honoring your grind.

Some lessons come from books.
Some come from school.

But the ones that stick — the ones that shape your DNA — come from moments you never forget.

For me, that moment was riding in the car with my father one Friday evening. I was around seven years old. The sun was dropping low, the streets of Southern California were warm, and my pops had just gotten off work. That's when the song came on:

"Just got paid, it's Friday night..."
— *Johnny Kemp*

I turned to him and asked, "Dad, what does that mean?"

He didn't complicate it.
    He didn't sermonize it.
    He broke it down in a way a young boy could understand:

"It means you work hard all week, and when you get paid, you treat yourself.

You enjoy the fruits of your labor."
That one line stayed with me for life.

HARD WORK IS IMPORTANT
— BUT SO IS REWARD

My dad was a postal worker, a car salesman, a realtor, and honestly a master at anything he put his hands on. No matter how many jobs he juggled, he always made time for enjoyment.

He taught me that rest isn't weakness.
Joy isn't irresponsible.
And treating yourself isn't selfish — it's required.

Because when you refresh your spirit, you refuel your ambition.

Growing up, I understood this lesson, but I didn't fully *practice* it. I was always focused on responsibility, on doing what needed to be done, on taking care of what mattered.

But as I got older, I realized something:

You can get so caught up working that you forget to live.

SACRIFICE WITHOUT BALANCE
CAN COST YOU EXPERIENCES

For years, especially as a young father, I sacrificed trips, memories, and experiences because I was focused on providing stability for my daughter. I don't regret taking care of her — that was never up for debate.

But I do wish I had experienced more of life along the way.

There are certain memories you can only make when you're young, certain experiences that shape your worldview, certain moments that broaden you. And as a Black man, those experiences matter. They build confidence. They open your mind. They remind you that life is bigger than your zip code.

I spent a long time in grind mode — no vacations, few breaks, all gas, no balance. And even though it helped me accomplish things, it cost me some experiences I wish I'd had sooner.

LOVE REINTRODUCED ME TO LIVING

When I met my wife, all of this changed.

With her, I finally slowed down enough to enjoy what life had to offer. She opened the world to me in a way I hadn't allowed myself to experience before.

Together, we traveled to:

- Africa
- Europe
- South America
- Central America

We explored food, culture, adventure, and rest. We lived. And those memories reminded me that life isn't meant to be one long grind. It's a balance:

Work hard.
Play hard.
Live fully.

Life is short — but it's also long enough for you to enjoy it if you prioritize it.

YOU STILL HAVE TIME

One of the biggest lessons adulthood teaches you is this:

You didn't miss your moment — you just hadn't reached it yet.

Even if you didn't get to enjoy certain things early on, you still can
You can still travel.
Still explore.
Still treat yourself.
Still make memories.
Still experience joy.

It's not about when you start — it's about making sure you do.

TAKEAWAY

Working hard builds your foundation.
Playing hard restores your spirit.
Doing both helps you thrive.
Honor your responsibilities.
Respect your grind.
But don't ever forget to enjoy what you're working for.

Because life isn't just about achieving — it's about living.

CHAPTER 5

ALWAYS BE ON TIME

Core Lesson: Respecting time is respecting people — and respecting your future

Growing up, nobody sat us down and gave us a speech about punctuality. But we learned early that being on time wasn't negotiable — it was respect. Respect for others. Respect for yourself. Respect for whatever you committed to.

In our house, time mattered.
If someone was waiting on you, you showed up.
If you said you'd be somewhere, you arrived when you said you would.

And if you stepped out into the world looking unprepared or late, you weren't just representing yourself — you were representing the family.

As kids, we didn't fully understand it.
But we lived it.

THE CAU LESSON: "TO BE ON TIME IS TO BE 15 MINUTES EARLY"

Everything clicked when I stepped onto the campus of **Clark Atlanta University**, the greatest HBCU on Earth. That's where punctuality became real.

CAU had a culture: **being on time means being early** — fifteen minutes early.

Not five.
Not right at class time.
Fifteen.

At first, I didn't understand why everyone was hustling to class so early. That's when I learned something important:

Professors don't care about your "grace period."
They weren't waiting around.
They weren't babysitting.
You were responsible for your education.

Showing up early guaranteed you:

- A seat where you could focus
- Time to settle your mind
- No distractions from people walking in front of you
- The mental space to absorb the information
- A reputation as someone who took their education seriously

You can't learn anything when you're distracted.
You can't get ahead when you're barely on time.

Being early eliminated chaos — and created opportunity.

BEING LATE WILL GET YOU FIRED QUICKER THAN ANYTHING ELSE

Once you enter the workforce, punctuality becomes even more serious.

The fastest way to ruin trust, credibility, and opportunity is to be late.
The fastest way to earn respect is to be early.

When people know they can depend on you to show up when you say you will, doors open for you that stay shut for others.

Because here's what leaders notice:

- The person who's always prepared
- The person who's already seated when the meeting starts
- The person who's ready before the rest of the team arrives
- The person who respects other people's time

Being early makes you available.
Being available creates opportunity.
Opportunity creates momentum.

That's how careers grow.

"THE EARLY BIRD GETS THE WORM"

My dad used to say this all the time.

And like most things he told us growing up, it was simple but true. When you show up early, you give yourself:

- Time to think
- Time to prepare
- Time to settle in
- Time to catch mistakes
- Time to get ahead before distractions hit

Preparation isn't just an action — it's a mentality.

People who are early are people who take their lives seriously.

BEING ON TIME ELIMINATES STRESS — AND BUILDS CONFIDENCE

When you walk into a room rushed, flustered, or unprepared, your mind is already playing catch-up. But when you arrive early, you walk in with calmness and control.

You feel confident.
You feel ready.
You feel focused.
You feel like the moment belongs to you — not the other way around.

Punctuality is a form of discipline.
Discipline is a form of self-respect.

TAKEAWAY

Being on time is more than a habit — it's a lifestyle. It sets the tone for how you operate, how you lead, and how people trust you.

If you want success in your career, relationships, education, and personal growth, remember this simple formula:

Early = Prepared
Prepared = Confident
Confident = Successful

Show up.
Show up early.
Show up ready.

Because being on time is one of the quietest ways to stand out.

CHAPTER 6

NEVER QUIT

Core Lesson: Sometimes finishing doesn't look like what you originally imagined — but that doesn't mean you quit.

Growing up, we heard the same motivational lines over and over:

"Don't you ever quit."
"Never give up."
"Finish the race."

Those words sound good, but real life is more complicated. Sometimes life pulls you off the track. Sometimes circumstances change your direction. Sometimes you don't finish the way you planned — but you finish the way you were meant to.

People often judge what looks like an unfinished story.
But they never see the battles behind the scenes.
The doubts.
The confusion.
The fears.
The moments you didn't have the tools, the guidance, or the confidence to keep going.

And sometimes, you lose sight of your own journey too.

This chapter is not about pretending the path is straight.

It's about understanding that "never quit" has layers — and sometimes, pivoting is the most courageous version of not quitting you'll ever do.

THE CAU STORY — WHEN LIFE REDIRECTED ME

As I mentioned in Chapter 5, I attended the greatest HBCU in the world — **Clark Atlanta University**. And one thing about CAU: the motto is legendary.

"I'll Find a Way or Make One."

I didn't realize then how deeply that motto would apply to my life.

I didn't leave CAU because I wasn't focused.
I didn't leave because I lacked discipline.
I didn't leave because I couldn't handle the work.

I left because **life hit me with something I didn't know how to navigate** — losing my eyesight.

At twenty years old, everything changed. What started as a simple irritation in my eye spiraled into vitreous hemorrhaging. Blood touched my retina. My left retina tore. My vision never came back.

I was young.
I didn't know who to talk to.
I didn't know how to advocate for myself.

I didn't even understand the systems available to help me.

Instead of taking a medical leave — which would've protected my scholarships — I withdrew.

That one decision created a domino effect.

By my second semester of senior year, the financial burden was too heavy to finish.

Back then, it felt like failure.
It felt like giving up.
It felt like I quit.

But looking back...

Life didn't end my journey — it redirected it.
I didn't finish school, but I finished purpose.

I built a career.
I grew into leadership.
I learned to influence.
I bought my first home before 30.
I became a father.
I found my footing.
And I found my calling.

Clark Atlanta's motto had already been shaping me, even when I didn't realize it:

You can still win... even if you have to make your own way.

WHEN QUITTING IS THE RIGHT MOVE — THE CALIFORNIA STORY

There are moments when quitting isn't failure —
it's wisdom,
it's protection,
it's alignment.

I spent nearly 20 years in the wireless industry. That career eventually took me back to **California**, the state where I was born.

At first, I loved it.
The weather.
The mountains.
The beaches.
The desert.
The freedom.

California is the only place where you can drive from snow to sand in the same day — and I loved every bit of it.

But slowly, reality set in.

Work consumed my life.
The commute was brutal.
The schedule was draining.
The lifestyle wasn't sustainable.
And my daughter — the most important person in my world — was still in Georgia.

On top of that, the workplace environment turned toxic.
Promotions were going to people cutting corners or playing dirty.
Leaders were winning through manipulation, not merit.

I've always believed in integrity.
And I wasn't about to compromise mine for a title.

So one day, something in me said:

"I'm done."

I quit.
Not out of frustration — but out of clarity.

I left California and moved back to Georgia.
For six months, I drove Uber.

I hung my real estate license with a solid brokerage.
I hustled and rebuilt my foundation.

Deep down, I still wanted something aligned with my purpose.
Eventually, I found it — a career I love, in a company that values and respects how I work.

Quitting California wasn't quitting life.
It was **choosing the life meant for me.**

QUITTING VS. REDIRECTING

Here's the real truth:

- Not finishing something doesn't always mean you quit.
- Sometimes quitting is intentional.
- Sometimes quitting is the pivot that saves your purpose.
- Sometimes quitting is the beginning of your real story.
- Sometimes quitting is how God clears a path you were too afraid to clear yourself.

The key is this:

Never quit on yourself — even if you quit the path.

Paths can change.
Timelines can shift.
Destinations can evolve.

What matters is that you keep moving, keep believing, and keep choosing integrity over convenience.

THE REAL MESSAGE: I'LL FIND A WAY OR MAKE ONE

So which matters more — never quitting or finishing?
The answer is both.

But in a deeper, more intentional way than people think.

This chapter is a reminder that:

- Your path may change
- Your goals may evolve
- Your story may take turns you never expected
- And your timeline may not look like anyone else's

But as long as you keep going...

You didn't quit.

You adjusted.
You pivoted.
You stayed in the game.
You trusted your journey.

Never quit on yourself.

Even when life forces you to start over —
start again.

Because you can still finish strong...

Even if you finish differently than you planned.

CHAPTER 7

ALWAYS BE THERE FOR YOUR KIDS

Core Lesson: Kids remember presence, not phone calls. Love is measured in time, not talk.

For eight years, all I wanted was a real bond with my daughter. Something simple. Something natural. Something that didn't need permission, negotiation, or conditions. But co-parenting can get complicated when control becomes the focus instead of the child.

Kids don't need perfection from their parents.
They just need presence.
They need memories.
They need time they can feel — not just hear through a phone.

Growing up, my parents divorced when I was around eleven. Even with the separation, my mom never blocked my father. She never used access as leverage. She never made me feel like I had to choose sides.

She encouraged me to call him.
She encouraged the relationship.
When he called me, she handed me the phone.

But those calls?
I don't remember a single one.

Not because they didn't happen — they did.
But phone calls don't build memories.

Moments do.

I remember the car rides to L.A.
Windows down.
Air crisp.
Mary J. Blige's *What's the 411?* blasting.
Boyz II Men on rotation.
I remember him taking me to modeling gigs, baseball games, and track meets.
The smell of the outside air.
The wind on my arm.
The feeling of being with my dad.

Those memories stayed with me forever.

That's what I want my daughters to carry too — something real, something felt, something permanent.

GEORGIA CHANGED EVERYTHING

My father eventually moved to Georgia. When it was finally time for me to visit him, I was scared to get on a plane. Nervous. Unsure. But that trip changed the direction of my entire life.

I rode with him all day while he worked — real estate appointments, contracts, meeting clients. That's how I learned the real estate business at an early age. Those days taught me things my mother couldn't teach in the same way.

Both sides matter.
Both sides bring value.
Both sides build a child.

If my mother had ever blocked that relationship, I wouldn't be who I am today.
I wouldn't be the father I am today.
I wouldn't have the experiences and opportunities I have now.

When I think about that now, I ask myself:

Why is it so hard for some parents to simply let both sides love the child?

There are 365 days in a year.
I was only asking for 70.
Seventy days to be a father without restrictions.

Was that really asking too much?

WHEN PARENTING STYLES CLASH

As I got older, I learned something important:
Being there for your kids isn't difficult — *until the person you had a child with makes it difficult.*

My parents didn't have a lot financially, but they had wisdom.
They had love.
They had structure.
They prioritized experience over control.
But when you have a child outside of marriage, and the other parent doesn't share your values, everything becomes harder.

Not because of love.
Because of perspective.

Everyone parents differently.
Everyone loves differently.
Everyone values different things.

But here's the truth:

A child deserves the full version of both parents — not the controlled version of one.

When both parents get to be themselves...
When both parents get to pour into the child...
That child becomes wiser, stronger, and more grounded.

Parenting is not about who has the most time.
It's about who gives the most quality.
It's about maximizing the child's experience, not minimizing the other parent.

THE REAL MEANING OF SHOWING UP

Kids don't remember:

- missed calls
- court orders
- monthly schedules
- arguments
- legal terms
- supervised visits

They remember moments.

They remember:

- the smell of the car interior
- the music you played
- the laughter in the parking lot
- the talks in the driveway
- the walks through the store
- the little memories that you didn't even know would matter

Being there for your kids isn't about perfection — it's about presence.

It's not about gifts — it's about guidance.

It's not about control — it's about contribution.

And most importantly...
It's about allowing both parents the freedom to love the child in their own way.

That's how kids grow.
That's how kids win.
That's how childhood becomes legacy.

CHAPTER 8

DO WHAT YOU SAY YOU'RE GOING TO DO

Core Lesson: Your word is your reputation, your character, and your legacy.

Growing up, we all remember those little moments when our parents promised us something — ice cream after school, a treat after work, a trip if we behaved. And no matter how tired they were, no matter how long their day had been, they still got up, grabbed the keys, and made it happen.

Not because they owed us anything.
Not because it was convenient.
Not because they had the energy.

They did it because they gave their word.

One of the most important lessons I ever learned was this:

Do what you say you're going to do — because integrity matters.

Not perfection.
Not overcommitting.
Not people-pleasing.
Integrity.

Your word is your bond.

It's the foundation for trust, respect, and credibility — in your family, your relationships, and your career.

THE DISCIPLINE OF KEEPING YOUR WORD

This trait shaped me as a man — in parenting, relationships, friendships, leadership, and my professional life.

Nobody is perfect.
We all miss the mark sometimes.
Life happens. Circumstances shift. Things fall through.

But the goal is to be as consistent as possible with the things you commit to. Because when people learn they can depend on you, everything changes:

- trust deepens
- relationships strengthen
- opportunities increase
- respect follows you

Doing what you say doesn't just build trust — it builds character. And character opens doors talent can't.

HOW INTEGRITY BUILDS YOUR CAREER

In my career, I've managed partnerships with external companies — leaders who influenced sales performance, customer experience, and brand strategy. Some partners welcomed me immediately. Others didn't.

Some didn't value me at first.
Some didn't understand my role.
Some ignored my emails or brushed off my suggestions.

And in those moments, it would've been easy to give them back the same energy.

But that's not how integrity works.

If I said I was going to do something, I did it.
If they needed help, I showed up.
If I committed to supporting their goals, I followed through every time — even when the partnership felt one-sided.

Sometimes I'd get a "thank you," but no real relationship yet.

But over time — and this is the part people don't see — consistency shifts everything.

When they were finally ready to listen…
When they were finally ready to collaborate…
When they were finally ready to trust someone…

They remembered the person who always delivered.

That's the power of doing what you say you'll do.

It plants seeds today that grow into opportunities tomorrow.

INTEGRITY SHOWS UP IN RELATIONSHIPS TOO

This lesson isn't just professional — it's deeply personal.

Dating today is full of half-truths, curated images, and people presenting versions of themselves that don't match their real character. Everyone wants honesty, loyalty, and consistency — but very few are willing to become the type of person who gives those things.

If you want a partner who listens, you must listen.
If you want a partner who is reliable, you must be reliable.
If you want a partner who follows through, you must follow through.
Your relationship can only be as strong as the integrity you both give to it.

Being who you say you are is one of the easiest ways to love someone.

Pretending is temporary.
Integrity is permanent.

YOUR WORD IS YOUR REPUTATION

Here's a truth that follows you everywhere:

**Your reputation is never built on what you *intend* to do.
It's built on what you *consistently* do.**

People may respect your goals, but they trust your patterns.

If you say you're going to:

- show up
- support someone
- finish the project
- keep a secret
- be loyal
- apologize
- follow through

then do it — not because it impresses people, but because it defines you.

Your word is your currency.
Spend it wisely.

THE REAL MESSAGE

Doing what you say you're going to do means:
- respecting others
- respecting yourself
- being reliable

- being intentional
- being disciplined
- being honest
- being who you claim to be

Every promise you keep strengthens your relationships.
Every promise you break weakens them.

In a world full of people who talk...
The person who consistently delivers stands out.

Your integrity is your legacy — and your word is the foundation of it.

CHAPTER 9

YOUR IMAGE MATTERS

Core Lesson: Image isn't just how you look — it's how you live.

We grow up hearing the saying,
"Don't judge a book by its cover."

And while the message behind that is meant to teach humility and compassion, the truth is something most grown adults eventually learn:

People do judge — and they judge fast.

Your image is one of the most influential tools you have.
Not just your clothes,
not just your haircut,
not just your physical presence...

but your **behavior**,
your **discipline**,
your **reputation**,
your **consistency**,
and the company you keep.

Your image is your silent introduction.
It speaks long before you ever say a word.

IT STARTED AT HOME

In our house, appearance was not optional — it was required.

Growing up, my parents instilled structure and hygiene into us early:

- shower every morning
- lotion your skin
- brush your teeth
- clean your face
- comb your hair
- iron your clothes
- look presentable even for quick errands

My parents drilled into us that when you walk out that door, you represent:

- your name,
- your family,
- and your upbringing.

That became the foundation for how I view image.

HOW YOU CARRY YOURSELF IS EVERYTHING

Physical presentation is just the beginning.

As I matured, I realized your **real image** is built on the things people don't see on the surface:

- Are you dependable?
- Are you on time?
- Do you keep your word?
- Are you prepared?
- Are you respectful?
- Do you surround yourself with good people?

Your posture, your tone, your attitude, your energy — they all speak for you.

People pay attention even when you think they don't.
And fair or unfair, they will associate you with your environment and your habits.

A LESSON FROM HIRING — A BOOK WITH A POWERFUL COVER

Early in my retail career, **my store manager — a woman** — asked me to sit in on interviews for a new consultant role. One candidate sounded impressive on the phone — sharp, articulate, confident.

But when he walked into the store...
his clothes were worn,
his shoes were beat down,
his appearance looked like life had been fighting him.

I'll admit — I judged him instantly.

But my manager, a woman with wisdom, patience, and emotional intelligence, looked at me and said:

"Remember — don't judge a book by its cover."

We interviewed him anyway.

He ended up being the strongest candidate we saw.
Dedicated. Coachable. Intelligent. Hungry.

Later, I learned he was homeless.
One mistake earlier in life had completely derailed him.

What looked like "poor presentation" was really a man fighting for a second chance.

He got the job.
He excelled.
He became one of my best peers.

That experience taught me two truths:

1. Never underestimate someone based on appearance.
2. But also understand that **your own image will determine which doors open for you.**

Both truths can be real at the same time.

THE PRIME TIME PHILOSOPHY

One of the biggest influences on how I view image came from Deion "Prime Time" Sanders.

He said:

**"If you look good, you feel good.
If you feel good, you play good.
If you play good, they pay good."**

It wasn't arrogance — it was excellence.

It taught me that:

*   preparation influences confidence
*   confidence influences performance
*   performance influences opportunity

Even today, I apply that philosophy:

Before meetings, I prepare mentally.
Before presentations, I gather key notes.
Before calls, I ensure I'm grounded, engaged, and intentional.

Your image is not only what you wear —
it's how you show up.

MISTAKES DON'T DEFINE YOUR IMAGE — LACK OF GROWTH DOES

In my twenties, I made mistakes.
Personally. Professionally. Emotionally.

Some of those mistakes hurt my image.
Some of them cost me.
Some of them taught me painful lessons.

But I learned something powerful:

**Your image isn't defined by your mistakes.
It's defined by your maturity.**

You can rebuild a damaged image:

- with consistency
- with character
- with discipline
- with humility
- with growth

Your image only stays tarnished when you stop growing.

IMAGE OPENS DOORS MONEY CAN'T BUY

Today, I protect my image intentionally — because it impacts everything.

Your image determines:

- how people speak about you when you're not in the room
- how leaders advocate for you
- how opportunities find you
- how respect forms around you
- how trust builds
- how people follow you

The best part?

Keeping your image strong doesn't require money. It requires discipline.

Discipline in:

- how you dress
- how you speak
- how you treat people
- how you move
- how you respond
- how you manage your emotions
- how you carry your name

Your image is your brand.
Your brand is your reputation.
And your reputation is your legacy.

THE REAL MESSAGE

Your image matters — not out of vanity, but out of purpose.

Because image is:

- your presence
- your preparation
- your character

- your discipline
- your decision-making
- your influence
- your identity

People may not remember everything you say.
But they will remember how you carried yourself.

So protect your image.
Honor your name.
Move with intention.
And show up as the person your values raised you to be.

Your image introduces you.
Your character confirms it.
Your legacy preserves it.

CHAPTER 10

TREAT OTHERS HOW YOU WANT TO BE TREATED

Core Lesson: What you give is what returns to you.

One of the earliest and simplest lessons I learned in life is this:

"Treat people how you want to be treated."

It sounds elementary, but it's one of the hardest things to consistently practice — especially as life becomes more complicated and emotions become more layered.

This wasn't just a quote in our house.
It was survival.
It was structure.
It was how four boys learned to coexist.

GROWING UP WITH BROTHERS — THE FIRST CLASSROOM

Being the youngest of four boys, I learned quickly that "fairness" wasn't automatic.

You had to fight for:

- the TV
- a plate at mealtime
- turns on the bike
- and even just peace

My older brothers teased me, pushed me, and sometimes "bullied" me — but not out of cruelty.

Looking back, I now realize they were preparing me for a world that wasn't going to hand me anything.

When things got out of hand, my parents would step in and repeat the same message:

"Treat him the way you would want to be treated."

That forced my brothers to think about empathy:
Would *they* want to be excluded?
Would *they* want to be talked down to?
Would *they* want someone taking advantage of their size or confidence?

It became the foundation for how I treat people today.

TAKING IT TO SCHOOL — STANDING UP FOR OTHERS

That lesson followed me into school. I saw kids get bullied — not physically, but emotionally. That "back and forth" that starts as jokes but turns into real pain.

At my cafeteria table, jokes flew all lunch period.
But if someone became the constant target, and I could see the embarrassment in their face, I stepped in.

Not to fight —
but to redirect the energy.

Sometimes I'd crack jokes back on the one doing the bullying.
Sometimes I'd just shift the momentum.
Sometimes I'd give the kid being targeted a chance to laugh again.

It wasn't about being a hero.
It was about being human.

I knew what it felt like to be the smallest.
I knew what it felt like to be outnumbered.

Treat people how you'd want someone to treat you if that was *you* sitting at that table.

RELATIONSHIPS — LOVE LANGUAGES AND REAL UNDERSTANDING

Treating others fairly becomes far more complex in adulthood — especially in relationships.

As men, we often want:

- respect
- trust
- stability

While many women want:

- protection
- communication
- emotional clarity

Both are valid.
Both require vulnerability.
And both require effort.

A lot of relationships fail because people don't consider the *other* person's emotional experience. We treat people based on how **we** want to be treated, not how **they** need to be loved.

You don't have to adopt someone else's love language, but you should recognize it and apply it in your own way.

If her love language is **physical touch**,
and yours is **acts of service**,
your way of showing love might be:

- rubbing her feet
- giving a massage
- hugging her when she walks in the door

You don't lose yourself by doing that.
You expand love by meeting somewhere in the middle.

LEADERSHIP — TREAT YOUR TEAM LIKE HUMAN BEINGS

My father was a supervisor at the post office, and he used to tell us:

"If you want to manage people well, treat them the way you would want to be treated at work."

I took that to heart.

If I value work-life balance,
I must support my team's balance.

If I appreciate transparency,
I must be transparent with them.

If I want grace when life happens,
I must give grace when their life happens.

A leader who demands what they don't give will never earn loyalty.
True leadership starts at the exact same place childhood did:

Treat people how you want to be treated.

EVEN WITH ENEMIES — STAY SOLID

This lesson applies even when dealing with people who don't like you.

You don't repay negativity with negativity.
You don't respond to disrespect with disrespect.
You don't match their energy — you maintain yours.

Because:

- **your character is the lesson**
- **your behavior is the teaching moment**
- **your consistency is what changes perceptions**

You'd be surprised how many "enemies" soften when they realize you're not their enemy.

Sometimes your behavior becomes their mirror.

THE REAL MESSAGE

Treating people well isn't about being soft.

It isn't about being passive.
It isn't about letting people walk over you.

It's about being:

- grounded
- intentional
- self-aware
- emotionally balanced
- consistent in your values

Life has a way of sending everything you put out right back to you
— full circle.

So give respect.
Give mercy.
Give grace.
Give compassion.
Give fairness.

Because eventually, you'll need those very things returned to you.

CHAPTER 11

NEVER FOLLOW THE JONESES

Core Lesson: Your value comes from who you are, not what you imitate.

This lesson is one of the most important ones I ever learned, and it hit me early — long before I understood how deep it truly ran.

Growing up in the late 80s and 90s, most Black households weren't trying to keep up with anyone. Many were simply trying to keep the lights on, keep food in the fridge, and keep their kids out of trouble. So when my parents taught us, **"Don't try to be like the Joneses,"** it wasn't just about money.

It was about identity.
It was about authenticity.
It was about being comfortable with *you*.

But I didn't fully understand that yet.

THE CHRISTMAS THAT TAUGHT
ME EVERYTHING

I was in sixth grade — one of the last Christmases before my mom became a Jehovah's Witness and before my dad moved to Atlanta.

My friends had both parents in the home, and they were thriving financially. They opened brand-new video game systems, fresh popular sneakers, and more toys than they could carry.

Meanwhile, at our house, we got gifts — but nothing close to what my friends were showing off.

I felt jealous.
Not angry, not resentful — just wondering *why.*

So I asked my mom.

She looked me dead in my eyes and said:

**"You can't be like the Joneses.
Just because someone else has something doesn't mean you need it."**

Then she added something that stuck with me forever:

"It's better to be the first to do something in your own way than to copy someone who already did it."

At the time, I thought she was just giving advice.

Now I understand she was giving me a blueprint.

As I grew older, I realized the deeper truth:
She wasn't hiding anything. She simply couldn't afford what my friends had. And instead of letting me feel less than, she taught me how to think differently.

That type of parenting stays with you.

THE POWER OF AUTHENTICITY

The older I get, the more I understand my mother's wisdom.

Being yourself:

- brings peace
- brings clarity
- brings respect
- and brings the right opportunities

Trying to keep up with others brings:

- anxiety
- comparison
- pressure
- and false identity

When you focus on your own gifts, your own journey, your own style — people gravitate to you naturally.

You become memorable because you're not trying to be a replica of someone else.

THE ADULT VERSION OF THE SAME LESSON

As an adult, social media has made "following the Joneses" even more tempting.

You see:

- luxury vacations
- designer clothes
- five-figure watches
- dream careers
- picture-perfect relationships

And if you're not grounded, you'll start comparing your reality to someone else's highlight reel.

But real happiness doesn't come from copying someone else's life. Real success comes from being aligned with **your** purpose.

One of the things I remind myself often is:

"What's for me is for me — and no one else."

If a job doesn't work out, it's not because you weren't good enough. It's because that role wasn't *yours*.

If someone else gets an opportunity, it doesn't mean you failed. It means yours is still on its way.

Your identity, your pace, your path — all of that matters more than trying to keep up with anyone else.

THE REAL MESSAGE

This chapter is not just about money or gifts.
It's about:

- knowing who you are
- not chasing trends
- not compromising your authenticity
- not losing yourself trying to impress the world
- and understanding that your journey is your own

When you stop comparing yourself to others, you free yourself to appreciate and maximize what's already in your hands.

Your uniqueness is your power.

Your path is your advantage.

Your pace is your protection.

Never follow the Joneses —
because what's meant for *you* will always find *you*.

CHAPTER 12

NOTHING IN LIFE IS FREE

Core Lesson: Everything has a cost — either upfront or on the back end.

This lesson hits harder the older you get.

As a kid, it sounds simple:
"Nothing in life is free."
But as an adult you learn that this truth applies to **everything** — money, relationships, opportunities, decisions, and even shortcuts.

What's given to you for free always comes with something attached:

- expectations
- strings
- consequences
- guilt
- or debts you never agreed to

And what you earn on your own always comes with something else: **confidence, freedom, and peace.**

THE LESSON FROM MY BROTHER
AND THE CANDY BAR

Growing up with three brothers, we learned this lesson early.

I still remember when one of my brothers went to the store with some friends and stole a candy bar.
It was small, cheap, harmless-looking — just a piece of candy.

But when he was caught and my parents got involved, the message was loud and clear:

**"Nothing in life is free.
And if you take something you didn't earn,
you will pay a price you're not ready for."**

That lesson wasn't really about stealing.
It was about consequences.

It taught us:

- If you take shortcuts, you eventually pay.
- If you accept handouts for the wrong reason, it'll cost you.
- If you grab something just because it looks good, you may pay for it far longer than you enjoy it.

Even at a young age, I internalized the deeper message:
Some costs are too expensive — even when the price tag says $0.

HELP IS NOT THE ENEMY — MISUSING HELP IS

This chapter is NOT saying you should never accept help.

Everyone needs support at some point.
Everyone should get guidance.
And sometimes blessings come through people.

But here's the difference:

**Help should accelerate your purpose —
not replace your responsibility.**

Help should never be:

- a shortcut
- a replacement for effort
- a way to escape accountability
- something you ask for because you quit

If you truly need help, ask for it.
If you're avoiding the work, don't.

THE HIDDEN COSTS WE DON'T TALK ABOUT

As you get older, you begin to see how this lesson applies everywhere:

Athletes and Agents

If you're a young, talented athlete, agents will promise you the world. Money up front. Gear. Opportunities. Connections.

But that "free" money?
It's a contract in disguise.

You could lose your rights, your career, or the freedom to choose your future.

Dating and Relationships

If someone's only value to you is money...
there is a *price* they expect you to pay later.

And that price often costs:

- your independence
- your peace
- or your identity

Workplace Temptations

If coworkers encourage you to take "shortcuts" to earn quick money, you could lose your job, your reputation, or your future earnings.

A shortcut that pays $500 today could cost you $50,000 over time.

Government Assistance

Some people genuinely need help — and that's okay. But when help becomes a crutch, it prevents growth.

Temporary support should not become permanent comfort.

DISCERNMENT: THE REAL MESSAGE OF THIS LESSON

This chapter isn't telling you to avoid blessings.
It's teaching you to use **discernment**.

Before you accept anything, ask yourself:

"Will this cost me more later?"

Because the truth is:

- If something is easy, it usually isn't free.
- If something is fast, it usually isn't right.
- And if something sounds too good to be true... it probably is.

What you EARN stays with you.
What you're GIVEN depends on someone else.

And the greatest freedom in life is knowing that **you built your success — no one handed it to you, and no one can take it away.**

CHAPTER 13

IF YOU BORROW SOMETHING, RETURN IT BETTER THAN YOU RECEIVED IT

Core Lesson: Respect is shown in how you handle what belongs to others — including their time, wisdom, and trust.

Growing up with siblings, cousins, and friends, you quickly learn the truth behind this lesson. When you borrow something and return it damaged, different, or worse than before, it creates tension — and it reveals something about your character.

But this lesson goes far deeper than toys, clothes, or cars.
It's about honoring people and the things they invest into you.

CHILDHOOD LESSONS: SHARING AND THE COST OF CARELESSNESS

When you grow up with brothers, borrowing is a way of life:

- toys
- games
- books
- clothes
- bikes

And whenever something came back worse than before, it was a problem.

I remember letting friends borrow my college textbooks so they could finish homework. When I got the books back, the pages were missing, bent, or stained. We laughed about it, but deep down I felt disrespected — because *care* matters.

Borrowing something means:

- you value the person
- you value their property
- you value the trust they placed in you

When you return things in better condition, it shows you're thoughtful enough to treat what isn't yours with honor.

BORROWING WISDOM AND SUPPORT

This principle is even more important when what you borrow isn't physical.

You can borrow:

- advice
- encouragement
- mentorship
- opportunities
- someone's time
- someone's influence

But if you don't use the wisdom, acknowledge the help, or complete the project —
you've returned their investment damaged.

If your parents pay for college, the way you "return" that investment is by:

- focusing
- getting involved
- interning
- graduating
- and using the degree to build the life you dreamed of

That's returning their investment better than they gave it.

People don't need you to be perfect — they need you to be intentional.

THE NEIGHBORHOOD AERATOR STORY

Around the time I was writing this book, I learned this lesson all over again as an adult.

My neighbors and I had an unspoken competition going about who had the best yard on the street. We landscaped, fertilized, upgraded equipment — the whole nine.

One summer we decided to rent a core aerator together, splitting the cost three ways. My neighbor used it first, then the next, and I used it last.

When I finished, I walked over to return it and my neighbor looked at me and said:

"Hey man... did you forget something?"

I was confused.
He said:

"You gotta clean the aerator before you bring it back."

And instantly I thought, *He's right. I know better.*

That moment humbled me.
Even lessons you already learned will come back around to remind you who you are.

Returning something better than you received it is:

- courtesy
- character
- and discipline

And in adulthood, it matters even more.

IT'S BIGGER THAN OBJECTS — IT'S ABOUT INTEGRITY

This lesson applies everywhere:

If you borrow someone's car

Return it:

- clean
- with gas
- and in good condition

If you borrow someone's time

Show gratitude.
Follow through.
Apply the knowledge.

If you borrow someone's trust

Honor it.
Protect it.
Don't misuse it.

If you borrow an opportunity

Treat it like gold.
Do the work.
Make the person proud.

THE REAL MESSAGE

This lesson teaches you to:

- take responsibility
- honor what belongs to others
- give more than you take
- and leave everything — including people — better than you found them

Because when you return things better than you received them, people will trust you with:

- bigger opportunities
- deeper relationships
- and higher responsibilities

And when people know they can trust you, doors open.

CHAPTER 14

CLEAN UP AFTER YOURSELF

Core Lesson: Life gets easier when you take responsibility for your space, your mistakes, and your growth.

This lesson is really three lessons in one:

1. Clean up your physical space
2. Clean up your mistakes through accountability and apology
3. Clean up your life by constantly improving yourself

Growing up, these three things weren't separate — they were all part of becoming a responsible human being.

PART 1: CLEAN YOUR PHYSICAL SPACE

In my house growing up, cleaning wasn't optional — it was part of the culture.

If you poured cereal and spilled milk, you cleaned it up.
If you woke up in the morning, you made your bed.
If it was Saturday, chores came before *anything* — friends, cartoons, or basketball.

And my parents didn't believe in surface-level cleaning.
You had to get into corners, creases, under the bed, behind the TV — the real cleaning.

I remember one Saturday in particular when all I wanted to do was play basketball on the blacktops. My friends were already outside hooping all day, and I tried to leave the house without doing my chores.

My mom shut that down instantly.

Not only did I have to do my regular chores, she added more.
By the time I finished, the whole day was gone — the sun was basically down.

It taught me that responsibility comes before reward.
And that shortcuts in cleanliness lead to longer work later.

PART 2: CLEAN UP YOUR MISTAKES

As you get older, "cleaning up" becomes less about toys and cereal bowls — and more about relationships, conflicts, and emotions.

One of the hardest things in life is apologizing the right way.

A real apology is:

- intentional
- specific
- sincere
- and backed by changed behavior

Growing up in a house full of boys with a mom, sensitivity wasn't our strongest trait. But adulthood forces you to mature emotionally.

As a husband and father, I've learned how crucial it is to:

- acknowledge when I'm wrong
- apologize without excuses
- repair emotional damage
- and show my family they matter

Cleaning up your mess isn't weakness — it's leadership.

PART 3: CLEAN UP YOUR LIFE — CONSTANT IMPROVEMENT

The final layer of this lesson is personal growth.
Cleaning up after yourself means refusing to stay stagnant.

It means:

- learning something new
- improving your hygiene
- working out
- building discipline

- seeking therapy or counsel when needed
- removing bad habits
- and upgrading who you are over time

You can't control everything that happens to you,
but you can absolutely control the person you become.

Cleaning up is really about **making room for the life you want.**

THE REAL MESSAGE

Cleaning up after yourself is a lifelong practice.

It's:

- responsibility
- maturity
- accountability
- and improvement

When you keep your space clean, your mind gets clearer.
When you own your mistakes, your relationships get stronger.
When you improve yourself, your future gets brighter.

Clean your space.
Clean your mess.
Clean your life.

Everything else starts there.

CHAPTER 15

START WITH THE COLLAR

Core Lesson: When the foundation is right, everything that follows falls into place.

On the surface, this lesson looks like nothing more than a simple ironing tip:

"When you iron a dress shirt, always start with the collar."

But the truth is, this principle goes much deeper. It's a blueprint for how to approach life, responsibility, discipline, and growth.

Because just like a shirt, your life is shaped by the order in which you do things.

THE COLLAR: YOUR FOUNDATION

The collar represents the core of who you are —
your values, your upbringing, your character, your early lessons, your
history.

When the collar is ironed perfectly:

- the shirt sits right
- the shape holds
- everything else flows smoothly

In life, when your foundation is solid:

- your decisions have direction
- your relationships have stability
- your goals have structure

Your foundation is the part of your life you build *everything else* on.

THE YOKE AND BACK PLEAT:
LEARNING AND APPLYING WISDOM

After the collar comes the yoke — the part across your shoulders
— and the back pleat.

This stage represents taking the wisdom you were given and apply-
ing it:

- discipline
- accountability
- emotional intelligence
- consistency
- responsibility

This is the part where you begin shaping your life with intention.

You take the values you learned and start putting them into practice.

THE CENTER OF THE SHIRT: GROWTH THROUGH MISTAKES

Next comes the center panel — the biggest and most time-consuming part to iron.

This is where:

- your mistakes show
- your wrinkles are the most visible
- you have to slow down
- you tweak, adjust, and correct

This symbolizes the longest phase of life:
your journey of improvement.

This is where you learn:

- patience
- resilience
- humility
- the art of correcting your own flaws

Mistakes don't ruin you.
They shape you — if you take time to "iron" them out.

THE SLEEVES: MASTERY AND PRESENTATION

The last part of the shirt is the sleeves and cuffs.

This represents the part of life that others see first:

- your professionalism
- your confidence
- how you present yourself
- how you show up in the world

When you shake someone's hand, they may not see the collar... but they *will* notice if your cuff is crisp.

This is mastery — the part where all your inner work becomes visible.

WHY DOING IT YOURSELF MATTERS

You *can* take your shirts to the cleaners.
But when you do everything yourself, you notice imperfections others miss.

Same with life.

If you let other people fix your problems,
you never learn the process —
and you never learn yourself.

You miss the lessons that come from:

- failing
- adjusting
- improving
- and elevating

Just like going to the car wash:
you come home and realize you could've done a better job yourself.

Life works the same way.

MY GRANDMOTHER'S LESSON IN COMPTON

This entire life principle started with one moment in my grandmother's house.

I spent a weekend with her in Compton, and like every kid back then, if you stayed at Grandma's house, you were going to church Sunday morning — no debate.

I brought a wrinkled shirt and tried to iron it myself.
I struggled.
The shirt looked worse with every pass of the iron.

My grandmother walked over and said gently:

"Baby, let me show you something."

She broke down the ironing process step by step:

1. Start at the collar
2. Move to the yoke
3. Work the back pleat
4. Press the body
5. Finish with the sleeves

In five minutes, she had the shirt looking brand-new.

But what she really taught me wasn't ironing —
she taught me **life has an order.**

If you start in the wrong place, everything becomes harder.
But when you start with the foundation, everything flows.

That wisdom stuck with me forever.

THE REAL MESSAGE

Starting with the collar is a metaphor for:

- starting with your values
- building from a strong foundation
- following a process
- being patient with your growth
- mastering the details
- and taking ownership of your life

When you get the foundation right, everything else becomes easier.

Start with the collar —
and watch your whole life smooth out.

CHAPTER 16

YOU CAN DO IT (DON'T PROJECT ONTO OTHERS)

Core Lesson: Encouragement fuels growth, while projection kills potential.

There's a question we all have to ask ourselves:

Do we build people up... or do we project our fears onto them?

Most adults say, "You can do it," but their actions — their tone, their energy, their doubts — send the opposite message.

And sometimes, without meaning to, we discourage people simply because *we once failed* at the very thing they're trying to do.

This chapter is about breaking that cycle.

PART 1: WHY WE SHOULD TELL OTHERS THEY CAN DO IT

Back in the 80s and 90s, kids heard **"You can do it"** all the time — but we also learned early that encouragement alone doesn't guarantee trophies or wins.

You still had to:

- practice
- work
- build confidence
- and push through fear

Encouragement isn't about creating false confidence. It's about **creating courage.**

My Track Story: Working Your Way Into Belief

When I ran track, I wasn't great at first.
The 100-yard dash used to tear me apart — literally.

I was nervous, almost sick before races.
I'd get headaches, stumble out the blocks, and by the time I gained speed, the finish line was already behind me.

But I didn't quit.

Day after day, race after race, my confidence grew — because my work grew.

Eventually, I qualified for the **California State Games in Northern California,** where I faced the fastest kids in the region.

I won first place.

That win qualified me for the **Junior Olympics months later.** In that race, the kid who came in second behind me at the state games ended up **winning the Junior Olympics.**

Why?
Because while I pulled a hamstring the day before the big race, he kept working — and earned that victory.

I didn't place that day, but I was proud.

Because the real trophy was proving to myself:
I could do it.

Encouragement + effort = confidence.

PART 2: WHY YOU SHOULDN'T LIVE IN FEAR

Fear has a way of stealing opportunities before life even gives you a chance.

The Missed Cereal Bar Opportunity

In college, I dreamed of opening a cereal bar next to campuses — a creative space where students could eat every cereal brand imaginable, study, and hang out.

I shared the idea with friends.
Instead of encouragement, they projected their fears onto me:

- "That'll never work."
- "Nobody's gonna go to that."
- "It's too risky."

Years later, someone else built that same concept — and it succeeded.

That moment taught me something powerful:

People don't always discourage you because you can't do it. They discourage you because *they* couldn't do it.

The Missed Real Estate Opportunity

Right after the 2008 crash, real estate prices dropped to record lows. A friend came to me with a vision:

"Man, let's buy a few houses while the market is cheap. We'll sit on them, rent them, build wealth."

It was a smart idea.
I knew it.

But I was a young father and scared to risk my savings.
Fear won.

I passed on the opportunity.
He didn't.

To this day, he's reaping the rewards of that decision.

Not because he was smarter —
but because he wasn't afraid.

Fear blinds you from what's possible.
Fear convinces you to stay still when your future is asking you to move.

PART 3: DON'T PROJECT YOUR LIMITATIONS ONTO OTHERS

This is the heart of the lesson.

When someone tells you their dream:

- don't inject your failures
- don't inject your fear
- don't inject your doubt

Your story is not their story.
Your fear is not their future.

Projection kills opportunities before they ever get started.

The truth is, many people discourage others unintentionally.
They want to "protect you from disappointment," but in reality, they're protecting themselves from revisiting their own regret.

Encouragement, on the other hand, creates momentum.

When someone comes to you with a new idea:

- hype them up
- challenge them constructively
- share what you know
- and tell them they can do it — because they can

Everyone needs someone who believes in them before they fully believe in themselves.

Be that person.

THE REAL MESSAGE

This chapter teaches three things:

1. Encourage people genuinely

Your words can spark a fire in someone or extinguish it.

2. Don't live in fear

Every major decision in life will ask you to choose between fear and growth.

3. Don't project your limitations onto others

Your failures are not their boundaries.

At the end of the day:

You can do it.
They can do it.
We all can do it — when fear doesn't speak louder than faith.

CHAPTER 17

WE ALL BLEED RED

Core Lesson: Never fear another person — remember they are human just like you.

This lesson is about more than courage.
It's about humanity.
It's about humility.
It's about remembering that no matter someone's status, background, or beliefs —
we are all human at the core.

And the moment you understand that, you move differently.
You stop shrinking yourself.
You stop overestimating others.
You stop fearing people more than you fear standing still.

WHERE THIS LESSON STARTED: MY FATHER'S STORY

Growing up, my father and mother always said:

"Everyone can get knocked down. Don't fear anybody."

But it wasn't just words — my father lived this lesson.

He grew up in Compton, California, and in middle school he was chased home every single day by a group of boys who were bigger and older.
Every day he ran.
Every day they followed.
Fear became routine.

One afternoon, my grandfather saw him running through the gate again and asked why.
For the first time, my father told him what was happening.

Now here's the part that shaped this lesson at a deeper level:

My father didn't grow up soft. He grew up trained.

At my grandparents' house — even when I was a kid visiting — my grandfather kept:

- a **professional punching bag**
- a **speed bag**
- and a full training setup in the garage

This was the same equipment my father grew up practicing on. My grandfather believed young men needed discipline, strength, and confidence — especially growing up in Compton.

So when my father told him boys were chasing him, my grandfather knew exactly how to handle it.

THE DAY EVERYTHING CHANGED

My grandfather listened and then told him:

"Tomorrow, let them follow you.
Bring them inside the gate."

The next day, my father did exactly that.
He ran into the driveway like usual, let the boys come in behind him, and once they stepped inside...

my grandfather closed the gate.

The boys froze.

He asked them why they kept chasing his son.
They said they wanted to fight.
My grandfather said:

"Then fight him.
But one at a time."

And one by one,
my father fought each boy —
and beat them all.

All that training on the punching bag and speed bag paid off.
And that day, the running stopped.
The fear stopped.
The respect began.

But the real message wasn't about fighting.
It was about leveling the mental playing field.

Those boys weren't superhuman.
They weren't better.
They were just human — like him.

They bled red just like he did.

THE LESSON BEHIND THE STORY

This chapter isn't about promoting violence.
It's about understanding something deeper:

Never assume someone is more powerful than you.
Never shrink yourself.
Never forget your humanity — or theirs.

EVERYONE HAS A STORY: THE HOMELESS MAN

Years later, I met a homeless man who asked me for change. Instead of brushing him off, I asked his story.

He told me:

he went to college
graduated
became a CEO of a tech company
and then lost everything to drug addiction

In seconds, I saw how fragile life is.

He wasn't always homeless.
He wasn't always struggling.
He wasn't always broken.

He was human — a human who fell, the same way any of us can.

It reminded me that judgment is dangerous.
Compassion is necessary.
And humility is essential.

POLITICS, RELIGION, AND WORLD DIVISION

Growing up, there were two things we were taught not to talk about:

- politics
- religion

Not because they weren't important — but because people should never judge you based on what you believe.

Today, politics and belief systems divide people more than they bring them together.
But if two people sit down and talk — without the noise — they'll often find they are more alike than different.

Men vs. Women
Left vs. Right
Black vs. White
Rich vs. Poor

Underneath all that?

We all want peace, safety, love, opportunity, and respect.
We all bleed the same color.

THE REAL MESSAGE

This lesson isn't about fighting.
It's about understanding people — including yourself.

It's about:

removing fear
removing judgment
seeing beyond differences
and recognizing humanity in everyone

Nobody is above you.
Nobody is beneath you.
People struggle just like you do.
People feel fear just like you do.
People hurt just like you do.

And at the end of the day:

We all bleed red.
So walk with confidence, humility, and compassion — always.

CHAPTER 18

OPEN THE DOOR
FOR YOUR SPOUSE

Core Lesson: Opening the door is more than a gesture — it's a lifestyle of respect, emotional safety, and intentional love.

Growing up, we were taught certain things as boys — courting, chivalry, respect, and treating a woman with care. One of the earliest and simplest lessons was:

"A man should always open the door for his lady."

That teaching was about physical action:

opening the car door
opening the restaurant door
opening the door behind you

But as I got older, I learned something deeper:

**Opening the door for your spouse isn't just physical.

It's emotional, mental, and spiritual.**
It's symbolic of how you show up in the relationship.

COURTING DOESN'T END AFTER MARRIAGE

Courting isn't just about the beginning — flowers, restaurants, long conversations, and physical gestures.

True courting is what you do **after** you choose each other.

It means:

- showing your spouse they matter
- prioritizing connection
- making space for their voice
- showing emotional maturity
- creating a safe environment for communication

Opening the door is symbolic of **opening yourself**.

WHY OPENING THE DOOR EMOTIONALLY MATTERS

People want to open up —
but they don't always feel safe doing it.

Your spouse might hesitate to share because:

- they don't want to be judged
- they don't want to trigger an argument
- they don't want their vulnerability thrown back at them
- they don't want to feel dismissed

My mother always taught me:

"Be careful what comes out of your mouth in an argument. Some words you can't take back."

That became one of the most important lessons in my marriage.

Because once you say something damaging to your spouse, you don't just close the door —
you lock it.

That's why opening the door is about:

- listening without reacting
- slowing down
- thinking before responding
- giving your spouse space to be honest

When someone feels emotionally safe, they walk through that door willingly.

WHAT MEN WANT VS. WHAT WOMEN WANT (GENERALLY SPEAKING)

Most men want:

- respect
- peace
- trust
- belief that everything will work out
- a partner who stands with them, not against them

Most women want:

- emotional safety
- protection
- to be heard

- partnership
- reassurance and consistency

When we forget these needs, we clash.
When we honor them, we connect.

This is why "opening the door" matters —
because it meets emotional needs in ways that words alone cannot.

A REAL STORY — TWO PEOPLE, ONE DOOR, BUT NEITHER OPENED IT

A close friend of mine married young.
They had a daughter and were living up north with her parents in the same home.

Although the intention was to help the young couple, the environment didn't give them space to become a team.

My friend had a dream:
Move south. Build their own life. Start fresh.

He moved first, believing she would follow soon after.
But she didn't.

Not because she didn't love him —
but because she didn't feel emotionally safe enough to make the leap.

She relied heavily on her parents' stability.
He didn't fully understand her fears.
She didn't fully understand his vision.

Nobody was wrong —
they simply couldn't open the emotional door for each other.

Without that openness,
the marriage fell apart.

Not because of distance,
but because neither felt safe enough to walk through the door the other
needed opened.

OPENING THE DOOR GOES BOTH WAYS

Opening the door for your spouse is not about:

- gender roles
- old-fashioned expectations
- who pays
- who leads
- who submits

It's about **love roles**:

- patience
- vulnerability
- grace
- emotional effort
- partnership
- maturity

It means:

- creating safe space for feelings
- supporting dreams
- resolving conflict with intention
- listening without defensiveness
- showing love through actions, not just words

Every time you open a door for your spouse —
physically or emotionally — you send the message:

"I choose you. I see you. I value you."

THE REAL MESSAGE

Opening the door for your spouse isn't about chivalry.
It's about intentional love.

It means:

- opening space for vulnerability
- opening room for honesty
- opening your heart to understand
- opening your mind to grow
- opening your patience
- opening the relationship to healthier communication

If both partners keep the door open —

- the relationship grows
- the trust deepens
- the connection strengthens
- the marriage lasts

When one partner closes off —
the distance begins.

This chapter is a reminder:

Keep the door open.

For communication.
For grace.
For growth.
For your spouse.**

Courting isn't a season —
it's a lifetime commitment.

CHAPTER 19

MEET PEOPLE
WHERE THEY ARE

Core Lesson: Everyone is on their own journey — leadership, relationships, and growth all require understanding where people truly are, not where you expect them to be.

Believe it or not, this lesson didn't come to me as a child. It didn't come from the neighborhood, sports, or my parents.

This one hit **later in life** — and when it hit, it hit hard.

A COMPANY THAT TAUGHT ME SOMETHING DIFFERENT

I work for a company I genuinely love.

It's not the traditional corporate environment where people feel silenced, overlooked, or undervalued.

The hierarchy is flat.

You can pick up the phone and call the CEO directly.

You can talk to senior leaders without layers in between.

That alone teaches you a lot about accessibility, humility, and connection.

I started there in 2018. During those early years, I was figuring out:

- how to implement strategy across our retail partners
- how to influence results indirectly
- how to drive performance through people
- how to build strong partnerships
- how to cement my identity as a leader

Around that time, I started thinking about leveling up.

Not out of ego — but because I knew I had more value to bring.

Then one day, a peer approached me:

"You should apply for this leadership role. You'd be great."

After talking with my now-wife, I decided to go for it.

I knew someone else — one of my peers — was also interviewing.

That didn't concern me.
What's for me is for me.

We both interviewed.
Later, I received the call:

I got the job.

I was excited, grateful, and ready to step into the role.

But I didn't yet realize how this moment would introduce one of the most transformative lessons of my career.

THE CONVERSATION I DIDN'T EXPECT

During my first 30 days in the new role, I scheduled one-on-one meetings with each member of the team.

I wanted to:

- align expectations
- understand their goals
- connect individually
- establish trust
- build clarity

When I met with the peer who had also applied for the role, I expected a normal transition conversation.

Instead, he looked me straight in my face and said:

**"I feel like I should've gotten the position.
But you need to meet me where I'm at."**

His tone wasn't aggressive.
It wasn't disrespectful.
It was honest.

He was older.
He was frustrated.
He was hurting.
He felt overlooked.
He felt disappointed.
He felt... human.

That moment could've gone sideways quickly.

But I've spent my whole life learning how to think before I speak.
I stayed calm.
I listened.
I didn't take it personally.
I didn't get defensive.

I thanked him for telling me how he felt.

And the more I reflected on his words — "meet me where I'm at" — the more they stuck with me.

Because he wasn't challenging me.
He was giving me a blueprint.

MEETING PEOPLE WHERE THEY ARE DOESN'T LOWER YOUR STANDARDS — IT RAISES YOUR AWARENESS

That moment taught me something leaders often forget:

People don't always need motivation.
Sometimes they need understanding.

People don't always need direction.
Sometimes they need patience.

People don't always need a push.
Sometimes they need perspective.

When you meet people where they are, you:

- understand their emotions
- respect their humanity
- build trust
- reduce tension
- create psychological safety
- help them grow at a pace they can actually sustain

That peer who told me to meet him where he was?
I helped him earn his promotion too.

Not because I had to —
but because I understood him better after that moment.

Because once I met him where he was,
he allowed me to help him get to where he wanted to be.

LIFE ISN'T ABOUT TAKING EVERYTHING PERSONALLY

This chapter is important because most people struggle with this.

When someone expresses disappointment, fear, frustration, or insecurity, our instinct is to:

- defend ourselves
- correct them
- misunderstand them
- judge them
- shut down
- take it as an attack

But one of the biggest signs of maturity is realizing this:

**Most people don't need you to prove them wrong —
they need you to understand where they're coming from.**

Not every moment is criticism.
Sometimes it's vulnerability in disguise.
Sometimes it's growth waiting to happen.
Sometimes it's someone trying to communicate in the only way they know how.

Meeting people where they are is not weakness.
It's emotional intelligence.

THE REAL POWER OF THIS LESSON

When you meet people where they are:

- relationships improve
- teams perform better
- conflict decreases
- empathy grows
- communication strengthens
- leadership becomes easier
- connections flourish

Leaders who can do this unlock something special:

They don't just lead people — they elevate them.

Because people don't grow from pressure alone.
They grow from understanding, support, and clarity.

And none of that happens if you force people to operate at your level rather than starting at theirs.

THE REAL MESSAGE

This chapter isn't about accepting excuses.
It's about recognizing humanity.

It's a reminder that:
- everyone has a story
- everyone has insecurities
- everyone has fears
- everyone has pride
- everyone has wounds
- everyone has a journey you know nothing about

Meeting someone where they are simply means:

**"I see you. I hear you. I understand you.
And I'm willing to walk beside you until you're ready to move forward."**

That's leadership.
That's emotional maturity.
That's connection.
That's growth.

Because life isn't about forcing people forward —
it's about supporting them until they choose to move.

CHAPTER 20

INSPECT WHAT YOU EXPECT

Core Lesson: Expectations mean nothing without accountability, clarity, and consistent follow-up — in leadership, relationships, and life.

"Inspect what you expect" was one of the first true leadership lessons I ever learned.

As an individual contributor, your world is simple:
You create your plan.
You execute your plan.
You track your results.

But leadership changes everything.

Leadership isn't about **you** anymore —
it's about the **system, the structure, and the standard.**

LEADERSHIP: WHERE THIS LESSON HIT FIRST

When you become a leader, you realize quickly that you're responsible not just for your own success, but for:

- the strategy
- the culture
- the morale
- the expectations
- the performance
- and the consistency of an entire team

People will always add their own style — and that's a good thing. Individuality brings creativity, connection, and personality.

But alignment matters.

Whether the goal is:

- hitting monthly metrics
- improving customer experience
- driving attach rates
- leading a district or region
- rolling out a project across partners
- scaling a process that impacts thousands

None of it works unless expectations are set with **clarity** and reinforced through **inspection**.

Because here is the truth:

**If you don't inspect what you expect,
your expectations become suggestions — not standards.**

CLARITY → ACCOUNTABILITY → PERFORMANCE

A team can't meet expectations that aren't:

- Clear
- Direct
- Uncomplicated
- Reinforced
- Measured

People don't fail because they aren't capable — they fail because leaders assume expectations were understood when they weren't.

Most performance issues come from:

- unclear direction
- inconsistent messaging
- lack of follow-up
- assumptions instead of communication
- expectations that were "felt" but never spoken

When expectations are clear:

- people execute better
- excuses disappear
- ownership increases
- coaching becomes easier
- trust grows

When expectations are unclear:

- frustration grows

- alignment breaks
- morale suffers
- mistakes multiply
- resentment builds

Inspection isn't micromanagement.
Inspection is leadership.

THIS LESSON GOES FAR BEYOND WORK

This principle applies everywhere — parenting, relationships, friendships, school, and personal goals.

Parenting: Kids Rise to the Clarity You Give

Children respond to structure.

If you want:

- chores done
- homework completed
- respect shown
- responsibilities met

...you must provide:

- clear expectations
- consistent follow-up
- accountability that matches the instruction

Kids thrive in consistency, not confusion.

Relationships: Most Conflict Comes From Unspoken Expectations

This is where the principle matters most.

People assume their partner should "just know."
They expect behavior they never communicated.
They get upset about standards they never expressed.
They hold someone accountable to rules that were never discussed.

You can't expect what you won't inspect.
And you can't inspect what you never communicated.

Healthy relationships are built on:

- clarity
- conversation
- consistency
- honesty
- vulnerability
- shared standards

You can't be upset about doors your partner didn't walk through if you never opened them in the first place.

Personal Goals: Hold Yourself to the Same Standard

Inspecting what you expect isn't just outward — it's internal.

If you say:

- "I'm going to finish school" → inspect the effort.
- "I'm going to lose weight" → inspect the habits.
- "I'm going to save money" → inspect the spending.
- "I'm going to get a promotion" → inspect the preparation.
- "I'm going to write this book" → inspect the discipline.

You can't grow from intentions alone.
You grow from **self-inspection**.

Dreams die when they aren't evaluated.
Goals fail when they aren't monitored.
Discipline weakens when you stop checking in on yourself.

Self-inspection is what brings self-expectations to life.

THE REAL MESSAGE

Setting expectations is step one.
Inspecting what you expect is what turns expectations into reality.

This chapter is a reminder to:

- be clear
- be intentional
- be consistent
- be accountable
- be engaged
- be present
- be involved

Whether you're leading a team, loving your spouse, raising children, or improving yourself...

**You don't get the results you casually expect —
you get the results you consistently inspect.**

CHAPTER 21

FINISH STRONG

Core Lesson: Own your failures, correct your path, walk in humility, and commit to finishing strong in every area of your life — no matter where you started.

This final lesson is not about perfection.
It's not about pretending you've always made the right decisions.
And it's not about showcasing a life free of mistakes.

It's about something deeper:

- ownership
- humility
- courage
- and finishing what you were designed to finish

No matter where you started...
No matter what decisions you've made...
No matter how many times you've fallen, or drifted, or been broken...

If you are still breathing, you still have time to finish strong.

Your story is not over.

Your ending has not been written.
And everything in the middle is still yours to shape.

FINISHING STRONG STARTS WITH HONESTY

You cannot finish strong if you are afraid to tell yourself the truth.

You must be willing to face:

- the choices that slowed you down
- the patterns that held you back
- the habits that hurt you
- the people you've hurt
- the pride that cost you
- the moments you avoided accountability
- the areas where you fell short

You can't fix what you won't face.

Humility is the foundation of growth.
Accountability is the engine.
Honesty is the ignition.

When you own your failures, you remove their power to control your future.

CORRECTING YOUR PATH REQUIRES COURAGE

Once you admit where you've gone wrong, the next step is correcting it.

That takes strength.

Correction means:

- apologizing where necessary
- rebuilding where possible
- healing where you're wounded
- cutting off what drains your spirit
- changing habits that no longer serve you
- getting serious about your growth
- forgiving yourself
- pushing forward even when the past tries to pull you back

Correcting your path doesn't weaken you —
it proves you're ready for the version of life that's waiting.

You cannot finish strong if you're too proud to start over.

YOUR LIFE ISN'T FINISHED — THE MIDDLE IS WHAT MATTERS MOST

You only get two guaranteed moments in life:
the moment you're born and the moment you die.

Everything in between — the middle — is where your greatness is built.

The middle is where you:

- stumble
- learn
- fail
- restart

- grow
- evolve
- heal
- rebuild
- and rewrite your story

Maybe the beginning of your life was messy.
Maybe the middle has been confusing.
But the ending?
That's yours to write.

And it can still be powerful.
It can still be inspiring.
It can still be redeeming.

You still have time to finish strong in:

- your relationships
- your marriage
- your parenting
- your career
- your character
- your spiritual life
- your leadership
- your purpose

As long as you have breath, you have opportunity.

WE ALL NEED A PUSH — AND THAT'S WHY THIS BOOK EXISTS

You're not reading this because life has been perfect.
You're reading this because you're human.

And I didn't write this book because I've done everything right.
I wrote it because I've done enough wrong to learn from it — and
enough right to share it.

Like you, I am:

- flawed
- evolving
- growing
- learning
- adjusting
- pushing
- believing
- and becoming

These 21 lessons are not commandments.
They are reminders.
They are fuel.
They are guidance for anyone who wants to take ownership of their story and finish strong.

I wrote this book for us.

GIVE YOUR BEST — EVEN WHEN YOU DON'T FEEL LIKE YOUR BEST IS ENOUGH

Finishing strong doesn't mean you'll always feel motivated.
It doesn't mean you'll always feel confident.
It doesn't mean you won't feel tired, discouraged, or unsure.

But give your best anyway.

Because your best is not measured by:

- how confident you feel
- how perfect you are
- how fast you move

Your best is measured by:

- your consistency

- your integrity
- your effort
- your character
- your resilience
- and how others experience your presence

Many times, people see strength in you that you haven't yet recognized.

Finishing strong is how you bring that strength to life.

THE REAL MESSAGE

This final chapter is simple — but powerful:

Own your story.
Correct your course.
Walk with humility.
And finish strong.

No matter what happened before today...
No matter how many times you've fallen...
No matter what you've been through...

You still have time.

Your story is still unfolding.
Your greatness is still developing.
Your ending is still unwritten.

And every new day is another chance
to finish strong.

CLOSING SECTION

There comes a moment in every person's life when you stop running from who you were and start running toward who you're meant to be.

These 21 lessons were the compass I used to get through childhood, mistakes, setbacks, success, heartbreak, fatherhood, leadership, and every moment in between.

And now I pass them to you — not as rules, but as reminders.

Reminders that:

- You can change your life at any time.
- You are not defined by your past.
- You are allowed to become better.
- You are worthy of the life you imagine.
- And you owe it to yourself to finish strong.

Take these lessons.
Use them.
Pass them on.

Your story continues the moment you decide it does.

www.ingramcontent.com/pod-product-compliance
Lightning Source LLC
Chambersburg PA
CBHW051626120626
46551CB00014B/1947